BUS POEMS

BUS POEMS

GARY ASPENBERG

Broken Moon Press • Seattle

Thanks to the following publications, where some of these poems first appeared: *Blackberry, Images, Second Growth,* and *Vol. No.*

Printed in the United States of America.

10 9 8 7 6 5 4 3 2 1

ISBN 0-913089-34-6
Library of Congress Catalog Card Number 92-75708

Project editor: John Ellison
Text preparation: Melissa Shaw

Broken Moon Press
Post Office Box 24585
Seattle, Washington 98124-0585 USA

To D.L., without whom . . .

Contents

BUS POEMS

Proem
(New York City to Atlantic City, NJ)

fate,
a matter of choice:
eternity or extinction—

the faces in the station
all wear the same expression,
dreading the miles to come . . .

then out
over 9th Avenue,
fruit markets, churches,
Voorhees Tech & the Croatian Center—

a long rising curve past the city,
under dark bands of bridges,
into the grey light
over Jersey, salmon sunrays
angling down—

train yards
and high tension wires,
an old furnace chimney
still standing
by brick-strewn hills—

marsh water,
dirt roads through the reeds,
tufts suddenly golden
in brief sun . . .

writing in our sleep—
dreaming of grasslands filled
with pipe & concrete pillars,
factories rising from
moonscapes of erosion,
their smoke,
like brilliant white flags
below dark clouds & orange light,
waving us on . . .

reddening sunrays
over low pine forests—
the light around the clouds
forming a fiery horse
that races beside us,
Logan's white horse of courage,
dissolving like sea spray—

it's the black horse of desire
that carries us
in its belly
down this road,
the lowering sun
like a drop of blood—

chain fencing,
silhouetted
against the top of the road bank,
divides
the town of my childhood. . . .

I

(Reading, PA to New York City)

for Vicki

darkness
is not just
absence of light,
but a condition,
equal to light,
a moiety
that we must learn
to move within . . .

a few red lights
float, drifting
as though through space
in the night before us—
a long, loosed
chain of diamonds
slipping down along the left . . .

I feel the movement of our lives
out there
on the highway,
a drowsy, lulled floating—

a perilous rolling,
rigid bounds
shifting in the dark—

you bring my hand closer,
within your
aura of warmth . . .

as we approach the city,
webs of electric light
spread across the meadows—

lights
and the reflection of lights
wheel slowly in the windows
like galaxies. . . .

II

(New York City to Reading, PA)

the world is flat
against us,
touching meaningfully
the senses—

the window bright and dusty,
crosshatched
with scratchings
as if something furred
has brushed by—

the Sun
's the iris
of a translucent eye of cloud
flat against us
with the brown meadows
and billowing white song
from valves & keys
of the great industrial
saxophone—

the land calls to us,
giant letters
sprouting from grassy slopes:
drink me!
smoke me!

the clouds filled
with their own suggestiveness
like the last reach of waves
into sand
or the skeletons of
fine-boned fish . . .

the bus hums monotonously
the only notes it knows—
autumn light
squeezing us,
beings of shadow
wrapped within
a Möbius strip
of sensation—

the lowering Sun
hints of golden fluids
over Pennsylvania fields,
fills closing eye-caverns
with a glowing scarlet globe
and dreams of metal
hurtling down on flesh—

an Amish horse and wagon
enters Kutztown
and one longs for
a real plurality
in this land—
individuals
growing fully
into spaces of mind and body—

the ancient countryside
glimpsed
within geometries
of grasses and
corn stubble,
lines of trees—
no machinery moving
on the healing land . . .

the Sun
settles,
exhausted,
gnawed by
grey mouse clouds—

the trees open
like empty hands
in fields
which begin to whiten
beneath the drifting snow
of sleep. . . .

III

(New York City to Atlantic City, NJ)

the constellation of
the Jet
rises
over Newark Airport—

burning bushes
speak in tongues of flame
on refinery grounds—

the lights
out of New York
reflect in black windows,
stretch away into space
like some
galactic carousel
spinning
out of control
back down onto Earth . . .

on a drive-in screen
a car
hurtles down a highway—
our imaginings projected
over the landscape,
our works
obsessively reflecting
our works—

the roads are images
of our selves:
fearful tunnelings
through the savage night
of the forests . . .

occasional angles of
porch or windowlight,
dark houses
among roadside trees
open
on Jersey flatland
to the night sky:
an inverted pyramid
    weighing down
        on each . . .

I try to locate
within my skull
a black egg,
tightly swirling emptiness,
opening
for the universe
to sing through . . .

shadows knife
across the seat before me,
hoisted guillotines
of darkness—

the windows steam over,
lights fewer,
farther away
in the woods—

the reading lights now
like little suns,
halos
funneling down
like grace. . . .

IV

(Atlantic City, NJ to New York City)

morning,
heading North—

the Sun
flashes through winter pines
& oak, strobes
white & red
across closed eyeskin—

bus space warm,
veined
with stale smoke,
sealed off
from surrounding flow—

sun & shadow,
a flicker like
firelight over
mounds of hair
nodding & swaying
almost
in unison . . .

the transmission groans,
dragging us
into day,
rolling North
as the Earth
rolls East—

Lévi-Strauss finds
one Myth
endlessly spun out,
transformed,
the Earth spinning
within/according to
some principle
of endless improvisation—

one theme
obsessively repeated,
varied,
like these
countless scrub pines
feathering
their scratchy gills
into the low sky—

their shadows
recede
on the hillsides
and stretch out again—
as our own
auras
of energy
contract
and expand
in tidal pulse . . .

riders dozing,
tugged relentlessly
across the morning
out of
their inner night—
minds caught in
the round of
change
& repetition,
chambered nautilus
of sleep—

then
a flurry
of wings!
the bus
suddenly filled
with swirling flocks
of shadow-crows!

V

(New York City to Freehold, NJ)

the Hudson grey,
congested with ice—
Newark Airport
a thin field of snow—

tufts of brown grass
like stiffened paintbrushes—
birds down
on the icy meadow—
only machines moving . . .

steam rises
from waters heated
in the industrial intestines,
like mist over
spring lakes at dawn—

bur Winter opens before us,
a glacier
crawling down
from the poles of consciousness . . .

easy to feel
the genetic concern
for the land, the urge
to ritualize the seasons—

the Earth here is dead,
skeletons of shrubs, trees—
this could continue,
these corpses
never green again . . .

enough
to make you fall down
within your heart
and cry for Spring,
coax it
with song and sacrifice—
give Winter
the death
it claims—

let it fade, snowy,
shambling off into
the forests of memory
like some great bear
to sleep

until its hunger
stirs again. . . .

VI

(New York City to Reading, PA)

drunk with sleep,
a lifetime of it—

power shovel
on squat legs,
a scorpion,
upthrust tail
stinging bruised
Manhattan earth—

high old fortress walls
at tunnel exit—
then horizon
stumbles quickly back
over scattered mounds of brick—

tug
moving downriver
alone—

brief exultation of
sun-glitter
on leaden Hudson
and long, flutelike lines
of marsh channels—

radio tower
down
in reeds and brown water,
two trees over
in Sunday's storm—
a weary song
as Spring
struggles through torn
Jersey wetlands . . .

it's the entire being
needs inspiration,
not just head
or heart—
each part
its different lessons—

the world flickering
into invisibility
along the edges
of our senses—
where a new world opens
in new colors . . .

the riding
settles slowly
onto the erotic surface
of the globe of dream,
sphere of cloudy fluids
turning
like Venus
in inner space—

a great, slow wave
of sleep
rises
from the rolling
farmland . . .

in the yard,
the dog lies,
old and fat,
on his chain
in the sun,
penis flopped on the warm ground. . . .

VII: Hyperdrive

(New York City to Atlantic City, NJ)

for Grace Slick

clusters of white flowers
on highway shoulders—
rusted railroad tracks
snaking into marsh grass—
glittering endless traffic
over Passaic bridges—

in the old
Amerindian game,
the three sticks
struck the rock—
trinity of cosmic forces
striking Earth,
starting the players moving,
the spiral down
& up,
cell code
to galactic swirl—

these highways
our spiral path
broken, intercepted
by local terrain—
reeds by roadside pond . . .

imagination cannot populate
the brown streams
hooking into & out of
overhanging trees
with their ancient peoples—
the Memorial Day flag
rising above the forests
is the flag of ball parks
and picnics—

the long, drifting rise and fall
of highway
moves on a different scale—
and motionless
within the riding
dark flowers of dream
blossom along the rows of seats,
and music wells within us—
bracken opening
under burnt-out stumps,
circle of song
rising through the angle
of the moment . . .

the highway begins to branch
with an infinitude of exits—
like summer foliage spreading
into Earth, into air, into
the intricacies of consciousness—

we begin to slow down
in holiday traffic—
when we finally stop,
this road will rise up, vinelike,
a multidimensional plant
bearing us
as its fruit. . . .

VIII

(Atlantic City, NJ to New York City)

night—
darkness
without and within—

bands of shadow and pale light
ray from headlights
over grassy shoulder
that becomes the flowing surface
of a turbulent sea,

the road a serpent
lifting us
along undulating coils . . .

we call to the Owl
as spirit of the night,
try to locate his eyes
to see through—
become instead entangled
in the arms of trees,
branches webbing the night . . .

living forms wait around us
to feed on
individuality—
each species
a different potential,

perspective,
available
to human imagination—
(identity
independent
of form)...

the road glistens
under sudden showers—
white flashes opening
a cavernous sky—

the bus rises steadily
along a plane
away from Earth,
into the night,
into
nothingness,
tires hissing

like wings
slashing sure
through dark forests....

IX: The Clouds

(New York City to Reading, PA)

curtains blowing
from apartment windows
under bus ramp—
a tug
pushing two barges
up river—
then detail lost
in the quickening flow...

the clouds
are mother-of-pearl,
bodies of
alchemical moistness
hazy
from the failures
of human imagination—

trucks pass
lettered Moon
& Sunshine,

Two Guys
(descendents of
twin Amerindian
war gods),

White Castle,
Old Dominion—
the past
fragmenting
the content
of the present—

names
drifting by
against the clouds—
bridges built
into time—

saying
we will
go through it all
again
and again
in altered forms
until it all
gets said,
realized,
the energies
find their channels
back to source . . .

our roads
curving in on themselves
already—
we need no more. . . .

X

(Reading, PA to New York City)

the summer opens
in specific plants
along the roadsides,
adapted
to this
single zone, image
of what the land comprises
to a wandering
nation—

growth of images
collapsing
under accumulation
of detail—
though the cloud
really does
turn a wizard's
hawk-nosed profile
over the fields
of Kutztown

and three girls
sit on a rectangle
of backyard lawn
sketching,
searching out features
of land and mind . . .

farm buildings,
insular groupings,
look to each other
across
the deep potential
of the land—

cattle browsing
in clusters—
the land,
multiple,
purely sexual,
tires
of its human monocrop—

this road
leads toward
a pillar
of black smoke,
a genie
mumbling fiercely
in sparks
and strokes of
orange flame
as it rises
among the trees
by a river—

specificity consumed
in the heat of
on-going event—
there is a payment
we must make
of complexity
to move through
the lies
with which
we've fouled
our lives—

the cloud
piled high
with its own detail
in the lowering Sun:
a red coin
beyond hazy
wooded hills. . . .

XI: Marco Polo in the New World

(Reading, PA to New York City)

sailplanes
define the shape of
local sky
over Kutztown . . .

this long riding—
the fields
rising and falling
in seasonal mandalas—
hills detach, float by,
wavelike—

towns merge:
stucco gas stations,
yellow Firestone stores on Main Street,
Pep Boys, Sun Ray—
a '50s magenta & black Dodge
drifts in on the
cosmopolitan flow—

movie marquees flashing
bright messages,
screens opening
like rear windows
onto paranoid imaginings
of neighbors—
mysteries of the psyche
growing weedlike,
unattended
within these many privacies . . .

Earth's fluid image
becoming simultaneous,
events merging—
history a John Ford film
with previews for
Alfred Hitchcock—

Washington & Jefferson
plot the fate of
the Republic
as Union officers
order an advance
through the South—
Marco Polo, julep in hand,
witnesses the climax
from the front porch . . .

Betsy Ross
tries to persuade him
to remain in Kansas,
but, while professing his love
for the land, its sheep
and cattle,
he reminds her
that his family is larger,
includes as well the many Easts,
the Old and Ancient
Worlds . . .

he stands alone
by a desert ridge
at dusk—the future
approaching
in the light of
an oncoming train . . .
he ages
& disappears—a flying
saucer rising
from the spot
where the train
passes—glowing
with radiation—
and the sky
begins to
ripple
like
water. . . .

XII: The Nostalgia of Space

(New York City to Atlantic City, NJ)

the whine of the tires
is the sound of
a tree's limb
growing—
bits of voices hanging
like grey fruit,
words indistinguishable
but soothing,
giving a childish
comfort
in the night . . .

you used to want to
wander invisible
through every house,
visit each planet—
but our spaceships
find them empty,
awesomely
unlivable—

what other wishes
move about us yet,
transformed,
unrecognized—
what promises
have we signed
in dreams?

the night's body
is sensuous, feminine,
our eyes parched
in deserts
of utility—
the darkness washes,
heals them
like Christ's fingers . . .

there's so much
on the heart,
and one must travel
such long roads
to get there—

the passing lights
send my silhouette
a hundred times
across your sleeping face . . .

the land is flat,
the stars sweep down
to the horizon—
there's nothing
between us—
this space
is not a separation
but connects—

we move by feeling
through the poem,
through our lives,
through the vibrant
connecting spaces—
each poem, each moment,
a continuation,
building upon . . .

we remember the story
of the woodsman
who could hear
the trees shriek
as his ax struck—
the ball of lightning
that caromed through the window
around the family at dinner
and rolled harmlessly
back out—
and the local devil,
one of twins
born winged
who escaped out the window
as the horrified mother
smothered its brother
with a pillow—

these stories live
beneath the stars,
may be
the stories of
the stars themselves
come winding down,
partially understood
within the roar
of night—
or stories the Earth
whispers through us,
a universal sharing . . .

the tearing of tires
on concrete
is the sound
of the Earth
turning through space—
radio pylons
flashing red
across the flat meadows—
we try to give the Earth
a human tongue—

our dreams,
weighted with desire—
the rocket
in its launching silo
has a human body,
rending its uniform
in despair . . .

clouds
and reflections of lights
obscure the stars,
close off
space—
bright highways
crossing the meadows,
like the Milky Way
lain down
across the Earth. . . .

XIII

(Calais, ME to New York City)

for Vicki

love, too,
must be renewed—
the bus leaves
your car lights
behind
in twilight
Main Street traffic—

branches fill
someone's lawn,
half a tree
split
& fallen—
the seat beside me
empty . . .

strange now
to have been there together,
walking down the foggy
dirt road,
ragged treetops
like torn curtains
on either side—

woods
& haphazard fields—
no pattern
save whatever set us, too, down
in that random
particularity—

we break the old
inward-turning spirals,
no longer even a novelty
to the locals, save in
holding on
to what they've let
fall away—

trying to learn again
forgotten multiplicity,
the uses of the specific—
for "poison" we read
"medicinal" or "sacred",
for "useless": "unknown"—
our own bodies there
bursting into light
as we embraced . . .

now a long silence
germinates
between us—
may it become a field
left fallow,
renewing in its own
rediscovered rhythms
needed compounds,
balances—

may it become a space
we can return to,
the past,
as Rothenberg says it,
come alive
and in motion with us . . .

daisies
grow from the rock face,
experience
transforming stone,
the renewing energies themselves
transformed, made usable
through the Earth—

you asked
which is more important,
love or knowledge?
understand love
and it will teach us
all else. . . .

XIV: Prisoner of Second Avenue

(New York City to Atlantic City, NJ)

sun heavy on palpable atmosphere,
city fading into haze—
here,
where the sea's breath
draws in, thick & heavy,
we spin out our imaginings
of ourselves,
our potentialities
becoming actual
everywhere around us—

moving within
our own poisons,
no way out
but through,
to clean it all
with our own bodies,
wastes
transformed in dream—
brush thick again
at the base of
scorched trees—

torn loose
from the locale
whose image we are,
energies dispersing
& coming together
again—

we can only return,
again and again—
no experience the same,
no matter that the roadside
floods us
with green familiarity,
no matter how dense
the friction of impatience
to get through it . . .

this road
takes us from
our apartment
by Second Avenue
through the oak & pine woods
of Southern Jersey
to a theater and a play
about the city we have left,
as if it had become
a mask
we can't remove—

the past thrown everywhere
up against the present,
memory
making us aware
that our affliction
is change—

until the memory of change
coincides
with the changing moment,
which immediately
becomes deep
in itself
and in
our selves,
in our separate
intertwining
lives. . . .

XV

(Atlantic City, NJ to New York City)

searching for a space
to write,
but these many waitings
fold in around us—

the loved one
lost each moment—
our bodies rupture, cancerous,
hearts weaken,
souls fail to grow . . .

alone,
the ocean
rolling out of the fog,
waves rising
at the edge of sight,
cutting the sand
from under your feet,
water hissing
round the back of your skull,
a red disk opening inside
patterned like a sand dollar
along the lines of
its unfolding—

and the yard
defined by cats
drowsing in their favorite spots
near feeding birds,
vectors bounded—
this is our comfort,
embedded in known forces,
aligned with patterns
we will never understand
except they tell us
where we are,
our myths
& histories aligned
along these axes . . .

the bus becomes a cave
of sleeping prophets,
oracles consulted
in trances,
messages and questions
forgotten
on waking—
aligned in body
and abandoned to dream
in the dark,
the dark,
a river we bathe in,
tributary
of the river of death . . .

this waiting
is not
to arrive where we are—
the mind
won't accept
this place—
summer Sunday traffic
slowing to a halt,
the trees leaning out
into the headlights
like ancient masks—

the stopped cars fill
with the search for
consensual myth—tales
of airplanes downed on the road,
of fires—the process
continues
awake or asleep—

and closing my eyes
I see you in your womanhood,
a tall, slim vase
with a single full flower—
the traffic stopped,
and I'm alone
in my balls,
veined and weighty. . . .

XVI: Studio II*

(New York City to Freehold, NJ)

the driver calls out
the names of towns—
newspapers caption
the stories of these landscapes,
but we needn't read—
America, where
the ancient races
play out their mutual hatred
and a new race arises
therefrom—

land of ornamentals,
dawncloud pink mimosa,
scotch pine on sun-singed
highway shoulders—
geometric projections
overrun the land,
labyrinth
of wire fencing—
any configuration extrapolated,
pure, run through all
its potentialities
in framed space—

* Studio II is a computer program that projects input design to infinity.

the bourgeoisie dream
& imagine their awakened desires
are revelations
of an absolute order—
the heavenly city descending
as lawns and paved sidewalks
across the chaos
of the wilderness—

the road of choice, chosen,
plays itself out,
sees itself through
to its end, which is lost,
finally, in becoming
something else,
which it was
from the start—
the plaster virgin beckoning
from her niche
among the sculpted hedges. . . .

XVII

(New York City to Calais, ME)

the drawbridge lifts—
a sudden gleaming arrowhead of birds
wheels over the river,
flicks away—
lowering sun on haze,
the light a finer level
of what is—

Jenkins—Rama—Valli—
the signs roll in, become
a drowsy song—
black derricks hanging their
hungry beaks,
the wire fence closed across
railroad tracks into
grassy company yards—

pale grey waters swelling
into the belly of twilight—
lights along the horizon,
Long Wharf Cruises
bright for the night excursion—
the fierce attention
that maintains us,
alert shells,
drops away,
the tide
shifting . . .

the vast dark factories,
the dark homes,
a moment of transition—
song *is* transition,
all gone home—

haze on the meadows,
tall grasses
& clumps of shrub—
all
gone home—
the houses huddled down
among dark trees,
the last train gone—

the haze thickening
into ground fog
in the tiny graveyards
and golf courses
of Eastern Connecticut—
the night golfers
playing the silver-lit
streams and knolls,
playing the night itself—

the lowlands fill
with spermy fluids,
treetops are islands
on lakes of mist,

their arms uplifted
this deserted night,
their sweet breath
all around us—

the hump-backed hills
drift by like grisled whales—
we feel their power,
would plunge our lanterns
into their backs,
let them light our way
across this
dark sea . . .

we struggle
to stay afloat—
neon stars gleaming
at the borders
of the Land of No Surprise—

the child across the aisle
being coaxed into sleep
knows where she is—
the mind tires,
begins to digest itself—

she becomes aware
of the darkness
behind the rim
of the eyesockets,
sinking down,
as if into
a lake
at night,
drowning
into brain,
throat,
chest,
belly. . . .

XVIII

(New York City to Atlantic City, NJ)

sleek machines,
red lights on
slick roads—
Lemmy Caution bringing in
his Ford Galaxy
out of the intra-European space
of ALPHAVILLE,
stars drifting by
outside the windows—

these drivers
have all been watching
STAR WARS—
travelling the space lanes,
mercenary adventurers
in the service of
American Revolution—

shadows of space liners
waiting at Newark Airport—
the lighted refineries
like space cities,
colonizers
exploiting an alien planet—

the air around us
suddenly fills
with colored rays—
we're under attack!
they're coming in
from above & behind—
THIS ISLAND EARTH,
WAR OF THE WORLDS—
swirling life energy
locked into
psychic space suits
& projected in paroxysms
across our imaginings
of a world—

the space routes
are jammed at the toll booths—
our star log is written
within the heart
of a beast
too huge to know
in its total, outer form—
our ship
the microscopic bloodcruiser
of FANTASTIC VOYAGE,
point of consciousness
moving through the brain
of a dying body—

attacked by the
organic defenses
of the being we would save,
these are the creatures
around us—
this is where we battle
our selves,
where the sick man dreams
he must die
a natural death. . . .

XIX

(Dubois, PA to New York City)

weeds by the train tracks
stiff & brown—
light snow misting
the low hills—
winter sun pearly
in afternoon cloud banks—

the crane rests
by acres of rock,
digging for a treasure
already squandered—
each rise opening
into another
gouged valley—

the woods fill
with blowing snow,
trunks & rocks & streams—
the land is too complex—
VFW, Patriot's Bible Club,
the fatherland—not
the land at all
but an imagined family,
peoples seeking
in themselves
that
which lies beyond . . .

the poem
needs a miracle,
though we inhabit
the only one there is—
we should go down
to where the dark streams join
below spruce boughs
and pray
to our sources,
our maintainers . . .

lines of Christmas lights
dropping away
into the dark—
the trucks line up
along the range of hills,
their lights coming on—
and in the dusk
beyond the ridge
gathers
and opens
a space
of pure potential,
a continent of dream—

in our sleep,
we pray to ourselves
and our connections
with the world—

the Moon rises,
our old opponent, change,
turning our fluids, tidal,
as she turns the world's—
the night's reptilian eye
opening & closing
above the Holiday Inn signs,
flicking a dark tongue,
tasting the nation's dreams—

and the children cry
in the softly carpeted
living rooms of America—
though they can talk
on the intercom
to Santa Claus
coming to them
from half a world away,
he brings them only
toys & games—
and though they are made to believe
that this is what they want,
their bodies feel
the seasonal somatic pull
and ache for revelation,
the pure love
of their own birth . . .

the bus plunges us
into the night,
into silence—
the Earth spinning by outside
beyond our control—
moonlight on ice
rushing by
in the dark
beside the road. . . .

XX

(Atlantic City, NJ to New York City)

the lights define locales,
centers of life
distant and clear—
but walls are built
within the house,
between the members
of the family,
their accumulating privacies—
the skyscraper
in the dream
burning,
collapsing mightily
into its many rooms—

the night is opaque,
far from what we imagine to be
center—
only the roads lie open,
roads we must pay for
with every use—
and we haven't yet
learned their cost—
roads forged by others
from paths
forged by others, back
into genetic space and time—

and the road we are travelling
is not yet
the Path,
though that lies along it
at every point—
and the exits
are no exits
but continuations . . .

the lands is dense
and repetitively complex,
too much so
for us to enter,
move through,
light or dark—

the stars are wound
dense and hot
in the sparse winter sky—
radar bowls
scanning space
for intelligent messages
as news of the social world
arrives out of the night
over the radio,
red-lit pylons
glowing on the open meadows,
and fills with static,
unlistened-to voice
of the Sun—

the lights around us join
in a long
cursive script,
pronouncing themselves
in a sigh
that is also
their name—

we're afraid
to accept your gifts
America,
even free
their price is too high—
our days are not
our own
and you want our nights
as well—
you have to let me go sometime
cries the aging woman—
but we never told you that
they answer—

the words we want
wind deep
into sleep,
like seeds,

through
into spaces
not found
on the maps of this land,
though, like Bethlehem and Troy,
they lie across
the same continent—

we re-enter a region
of snow, broken
and crusted,
to inhabit at last
our own land—
and the dream
works its way toward
some place it yearns to come to,
a destination we do not recognize,
a realization,
statement, even
a pun, and
suddenly
stops. . . .

XXI

(New York City to Atlantic City, NJ)

puddles
lie by railroad tracks
where the ice
has melted—
the Sun,
day's eye,
closing—
all the shadows aligned
along
that axis—
white wings stretching
and folding
by shallow waters—

rusting metal, brick, shattered
glass fills empty lots
by tar-shingled row houses—
the thin clouds
prism the light,
lines of a bright text
over another
drab Spring—

sun on
channel water's
beaten surface,
spearhead of light—

the Sun itself,
Coomaraswamy has it,
is a door, Janna Coeli—
gleaming on rusted tracks,
on wings,
on water snaking
through blowing reeds—
upper door . . .

life here
loses its hold,
its cohesion—
Newark to the Amboys
dissolving
in dust—

it's not that words fail,
but experience
rouses only
associations,
attention
follows its own concerns,
furrowing
the landscape—

lights of the city
melancholy
on dark water—
we ride on, paying
by the hour,
by the mile—
the doors, standing open,
unentered—

night
closes our eyes
& throws us back
down the caverns of
the ear,
the sound
resonating
within,
drawing us
into real depth—

listen!
all the night-time Earth
turned inward,
listening. . . .

Envoi: The Third Song

the towers lie where they fall
in the marshlands of New Jersey,
painted metal tubing
like the framework of carnival rides
sinking into grassy waters,
the tides chewing at the form,
molecule by rusting molecule—
the ant-like procession of trucks
heaping mounds of corruption
on the plains between the cities—
the industrial lacework rising
beside the simple folds of houses—
tiny yellow tractors moving among the trees,
rows of storage tanks spread out
on flats scraped beside twisting salt creeks—
a continuous process—

the trees have come alive again,
the weeds again in cleared lots—
the land still filled with a people
seeking a living one more year
from their own inventiveness . . .

there is a song of the land,
the weed-filled waters below the dark trees—

there is a song of the work,
which rises from the self—

and there is a third song,
that moves between and modulates
the others—a third song
we must also
learn to sing. . . .

About the Author

Gary Aspenberg has published poetry and prose in *The Village Voice, Mother Jones, Poets & Writers, American Book Review, Visions, Tin Wreath, Lactuca, Vol. No., Caliban, The Colorado North Review, Verve, The And Review,* and *The Cape Rock*. He lives with his family in New York City.

Design by Nick Gregoric.

Text set in Sabon by
Blue Fescue Typography and Design,
Seattle, Washington.

Broken Moon Press books
are printed on acid-free, recycled paper
exclusively by
Malloy Lithographing, Inc.
5411 Jackson Road
Ann Arbor, Michigan 48106.